BRITAIN IN OLD PHOTOGRAPHS

HOLDERNESS

IAN AND MARGARET SUMNER

D1440042

ALAN SUTTON PUBLISHING LIMITED Y 942

Alan Sutton Publishing Limited
Phoenix Mill · Far Thrupp · Stroud
Gloucestershire · GL5 2BU

First published 1995

Cover photographs: (front) an Aunt Sally at a school feast; (back) holiday-makers on Spurn Point.

British Library Cataloguing in Publication Data.
A catalogue record for this book is available from
the British Library.

ISBN 0-7509-0763-0

Typeset in 9/10 Sabon.
Typesetting and origination by
Alan Sutton Publishing Limited.
Printed in Great Britain by
Hartnolls, Bodmin, Cornwall.

Contents

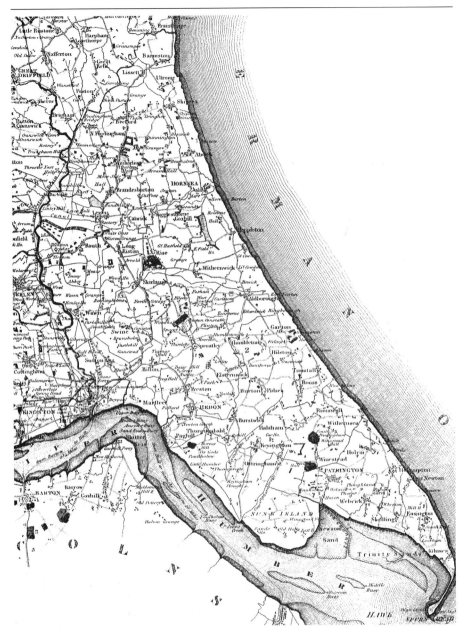

A map of Holderness, 1834.

Introduction

The area known as Holderness (a Scandinavian word meaning 'the headland held by a higher yeoman') runs the length of the coast of the East Riding, from just south of Bridlington to Spurn Point, around into the Humber to the mouth of the River Hull, then back north again along the line of the river. It is now an area rich in agriculture, but this was not always the case. The hummocky landscape consisted of small 'islands' surrounded by marshy hollows. These were once filled with water, and together with the marshy Hull valley, must have presented a significant barrier to settlement and farming.

The first settlements were situated on these hummocks. The low-lying coast of the Humber estuary made an ideal landing place, and Holderness was subject to waves of invaders, Anglian and Dane. The earliest Anglian settlements of the fifth and sixth centuries are revealed by their names – for example, Ottringham, Keyingham, Skeffling, Halsham. Those who came later settled at places such as Patrington and Easington. By the time the Vikings settled here, in the ninth century, much of the best available land had already been occupied, but there was still enough left for their farms – for these were not the horned-helmeted robbers of many a Hollywood film. Men such as Beorn, Wulfere, Brandr, Catta and Hrdolf built their isolated houses on the hitherto unoccupied poorer ground (and the settlements thus founded grew to become Barmston, Ulrome, Brandesburton, Catwick and Hilston respectively). Curiously, none of the invaders appears to have lived at Roos, which retains a Celtic name, meaning 'moor' or 'heathland'.

The Holderness landscape contained many meres even into the Middle Ages – place-names such as (Burton) Pidsea, Hornsea, Withernsea and Skipsea commemorate long-disappeared pools. There was a 'marr' at Sutton, an eel-pond at Brandesburton, a fishery near Burstwick and another mere at Lambwath. Most of these were drained, either by man or by the erosion of the coast. At the same time, the fields around each village were also being extended at the expense of the woodland which surrounded them: communities such as Swine, Bewholme, Burton Constable and Routh all had significant stretches of woodland in them; and names such as Woodhouse in North Skirlaugh, Woodhall in Ellerby and Ruddens in Withernwick commemorate new settlements carved out of the forest. Attempts in the thirteenth century to reclaim land on the Humber Banks came to nought when the dikes began to burst at regular intervals from 1250 onwards, and villages and farms were overwhelmed.

Ruling over the whole area were the Lords of Holderness. The first was Drogo de Beuvrière, who built the castle at Skipsea; from him, the title passed to the Counts of Aumale in the late eleventh century, before reverting, at the end of the thirteenth century, to the Crown. The Crown granted the title to the Constable family in the sixteenth century, and it has remained with them and the Chichester-Constables ever since. As such, they wielded considerable power and influence locally over law and order, husbandry and drainage. They could even influence building, for they also controlled the removal of cobbles from the seashore for use as a cheap building material; banning their removal from the shore meant that houses had to be made from brick.

Being somewhat off the beaten track, travellers coming to the area were not always impressed by what they found: Celia Fiennes refers to 'sad poore' Brandesburton in 1697; Abraham de la Pryme, a noted Hull antiquary of the same period, wrote about Swine as being 'very mean and inconsiderable, nobody inhabiting the same but a few country clowns'. Part of the reason for the poverty of the area was the action of the sea. At one time, there were several small ports on the coast – at Skipsea and Hornsea, for example – but erosion washed them away. Conversely, by the seventeenth century, two ports built on the Humber, Hedon and Patrington, were largely silted up. There was therefore little trade flowing through the area.

This state of affairs altered during the eighteenth century, when several schemes were put into effect with the idea of draining the Hull valley and the other low-lying areas by systems of dikes and drains. At the same time, work was being done to reclaim land from the Humber, particularly around Sunk Island. This opened up a large acreage to cultivation, and the area began to increase in prosperity.

As well as being known for its cereal crops, Holderness became reknowned nationally for the breeding of horses. These were not necessarily racehorses, although some fine winning horses were bred here, including the gallant and popular Nancy, after which the pub in Burton Pidsea was named. The main trade was in hackneys and carriage horses, and in horses for the army – though this was in decline by the end of the nineteenth century.

Not even turnpike roads to Patrington and as far as White Cross, nor the coming of the railway, could end the area's isolation. The railway was originally built to provide access to the resorts of Hornsea and Withernsea, which thus brought some business into the area. The improved transport system also made it easier to move agricultural produce out of the district to buyers in Hull and Beverley. This forced many local markets to close, and drove the tradesmen who relied on them out of business.

The scouring action of the sea had already eroded a good deal of the coastline by the time Celia Fiennes was on her travels. It is thought that the Roman coastline was some 1¼ miles to the east of the present one, and an average of 21 acres is lost every year. The port of Ravenser, built on Spurn Point, and bigger than Hull in its time, had been washed away completely by the end of the fourteenth century, and a further thirty or so villages have been lost to the sea since the time of the Domesday Survey: Wilsthorpe, Auburn, Hartburn, Hyde, Withow, Cleton, Northorpe, Hornsea Burton, Hornsea Beck, Southorpe, Great Colden, Colden Parva, Old Aldbrough, Ringborough, Monkwell, Monkwike, Sand le Mere, Waxholme, Owthorne Sisterkirke, Newsham, Old Withernsea, Out Newton, Dimlington, Turmarr, Northorp, Hoton, Old Kilnsea, Ravenser, Ravenserodd and, continuing into the Humber estuary, Burstall Priory, Penisthorpe, Frismerske, Orwithfleet, East Somerte, Tharlesthorp and Saltagh. Some of these villages moved a mile or so inland and started again; others were simply abandoned.

Much of the material that is washed away is deposited on Spurn Point. As mentioned above, the size of the Point was once sufficient to sustain a port, but it is always moving, being built up and demolished again by the sea. This is still happening: the neck of the Point will soon be breached, and eventually the island that is thus formed, where the lighthouse now stands, will be washed away, only to be replaced by a new spit slightly further inland – and the whole process will begin again.

NORTHERN
VILLAGES

Barmston post office, which at this time was on the north side of Sands Lane, at the eastern end of the village. The sub-postmaster was Alfred Ransome. Next door to the right was the smithy.

The Old Hall, Barmston, farmed by George Watson. This was the manor house of the Boynton family before they moved to Burton Agnes Hall. It was originally built in the seventeenth century on a moated site, but had largely been dismantled by the end of the eighteenth century. A range of more modern farm buildings stands to the north, and the village church is just to the east – some distance from the rest of the village.

The lifeboatmen of Barmston, 1897. Back row, left to right: Decko Smith, Henry Martin, Dick Purvis, Luke Smith, Isaac Smith, Frank Tallentire, Tommy Pickles, Mr Chauplin, Wes Jewitt. Middle row: ? Wilson, J. Acklam (Coastguard), J. Oldham, -?-(Coastguard), Richard Purvis. Front row: ? Harrison, -?-, F. Harrison, ? Clark, ? Fairbotham. The station closed soon after this picture was taken, and the lifeboat, the *George and Jane Walker*, was transferred to Bridlington, where it served for a further year before being sold.

The Rectory, Barmston (now called Barmston House). The original building was constructed early in the eighteenth century, but the greater part of the existing one was added, at considerable expense, in 1776 by the then incumbent, the Revd William Dade. The incumbent at the time of the picture was the Revd Charles Ingram William Boynton, who was a relative of the owners of Burton Agnes Hall.

Looking towards Manor House Farm, Ulrome. It was built in about 1785 by the Rickaby family, who were lords of the manor, using material from the old manor-house; the latter had been built in about 1637 by George Hartas, a member of a prominent Quaker family. The farmer at this time was Thomas Horner.

'Bridlington Road End' (as the original caption to this photograph put it, otherwise The Green, Ulrome), looking towards Ulrome Hall Farm. Just visible in the left background is the roof of the school, built in 1897.

Cliff Top Farm, Southfield Lane, Ulrome. Although some distance from the cliffs when this picture was taken, the farm has since been lost to the sea, and its fields are now the site of a caravan park.

Repairing Fisher Bridge, over Barmston Drain, Lissett, 1913. The photograph looks east towards Allison Lane End. The Beverley Barmston Drain was cut at the end of the eighteenth century to drain off water from the peaty carrs along the Hull valley. It was one of a number of improvement schemes carried out in Holderness between 1760 and 1830 which opened the river valley to cultivation.

The north-east corner of Skipsea, looking south towards George Cammidge's grocer's and draper's. Cammidge was not only a shopkeeper, but was also clerk to the Parish Council and assistant overseer of the poor.

The west end of Skipsea, looking northwards. At the end of the row of houses on the left was the school. The shop on the right is selling cycle spares.

The Green, Skipsea, looking towards the Recreation Room (right). In the left background is the Board Inn, run by Henry Gerrard. There may have been a small port at Skipsea during the thirteenth century associated with Skipsea Brough. This was a medieval 'new town', promoted by the Counts of Aumale, who also owned the castle there. The venture failed, and now all that remains are the castle's earthworks.

George Allman's cycle shop in Skipsea. The signs advertise New Hudson ('The World's Best Value') bikes, as well as Raleigh and Fleet makes. Cycling was a popular pastime from the end of the nineteenth century, and was a handy means of transport in isolated villages – sufficient at least to support this shop, at a distance from major population centres.

Cliff-top bungalows at Skipsea. The erosion of the cliffs prompted some farmers to lease plots in order to get money back on fields that had become too small to farm. Largely built from wood and tarred felt, the bungalows were used as holiday homes, although some were occupied all the year round.

North Frodingham. The Market Cross can just be made out in the background. It was erected in about 1811, and has recently been restored. The village had a weekly market until the eighteenth century. Note the decorative window frames of Commerce House on the right, with swags of flowers; the shop was owned by Frederick Swift – he was a grocer, draper and cycle agent, as well as the postmaster.

The completion of a wagon belonging to Henry Potter of Watton Carr Farm in a yard in North Frodingham.

Looking down West Street, North Frodingham. On the right is Park Farm, while Cross Farm is behind the wall in the left background. Note the contrast in headgear between the simple bonnet of the older woman in the foreground and the flowery confection being worn by the woman behind. Hidden by the houses on the right is the Market Cross.

Looking north along the Beck at North Frodingham. The swing bridge and The Gate pub (licensee William Allman) are just off the picture to the right. The buildings and haystack in the picture belong to Nathan Morris's farm, with the house just visible on the right.

Sheep-shearing by hand at Beeford. There are spare clippers hanging on the wall behind.

Looking westwards in Brandesburton. On the right is Old Manor House Farm, built in 1818, and on the left is The Black Swan. A seventeenth-century visitor, the well-travelled Celia Fiennes, did not like the village, which she called 'a sad poore thatch'd place and [with] only 2 or 3 sorry Ale-houses'. Nevertheless she was well entertained at the Manor House, perhaps because of her family connections. The Fiennes family, the Lords Dacre, were lords of the manor until 1611, when the title passed to the mayor and aldermen of the City of London, acting as trustees for Emmanuel Hospital.

Looking in the opposite direction to the previous picture. On the right is Cross Hill and Boardman Lane. The cross marks the site of the village fair and market. This had originally been granted in the thirteenth century, during the reign of Edward I, but, like those of Leven and Skipsea, became moribund in later times – it had certainly ceased by 1750.

The Dacre Arms, Brandesburton, on the left, while the other end of Boardman Lane is on the right. In the centre is a motor bus: the North Eastern Railway ran three buses a day each way between Beverley and Brandesburton, a journey of fifty-three minutes.

Lieutenant-Colonel James Harrison, the owner of Brandesburton Hall, and his wife, c. 1917. The hall was built in 1772, extended in 1852, and then largely rebuilt by Beverley architect William Hawe in 1872. It is now part of Brandesburton Hospital.

The cricket pavilion at Brandesburton Hall, 1917. Seated on the left is Lieutenant-Colonel Harrison, and standing in the centre is his wife. The clergyman on the right may be the Revd Canon William Vashon, vicar of Brandesburton.

Lieutenant-Colonel Harrison's chauffeur, Ernest Maddox, *c.* 1912. After leaving the Colonel's employ, he became a partner in the gravel extraction firm of Maddox and Matlow, which is now Hoveringham Gravel.

A row of cottages on Main Street in Seaton, on what is now a very busy corner. The corner of Butcher Row is just visible on the left. The shop on the right is now the post office, but at the time this photograph was taken Mrs Rhoda Thompson's post office was on the other side of the road, in a house which has since been demolished.

The Rectory, Catwick, rebuilt around an eighteenth-century house in 1862–3, at the same time that the church was restored, by George Wilkinson of Hull. The gateway in the garden wall on to the main road incorporates Norman shafts removed from the church during its restoration. The rector at the time was the Revd William Smith, and perhaps this is he.

Catwick village from the west, looking over Rowpit Lane, which runs behind the hedge. The sender of the card, who is identified only by the initials 'J.H.', has drawn a cross over the smithy – this suggests that the card was written by the blacksmith himself, whose name was John Hugill. The eighteenth-century Catwick House is just visible behind the trees in the background.

Looking south along the main road to Leven. The village occupied an important position at the junction of roads to Hornsea, Bridlington, Beverley and Hull; but the site of the village may have moved, since the original medieval church, St Faith's, stood about 1 mile to the west. It was perhaps the opening of the canal in 1802 that prompted this change in the village's centre of gravity. The tranquillity of the scene shown here was until recently very much a thing of the past. The opening of a new bypass has, however, gone some way to restoring a similar peace and quiet.

A gathering in the yard of George Bassindale's smithy near the crossroads. They may be discussing the finer points of the plough in the foreground, or how the unfortunate man in the centre came by his injury – or perhaps just putting the world to rights. The man standing on the left is dressed in traditional farm labourer's clothes – double-breasted waistcoat, corduroy breeches and leggings. The smithy was often the centre of the working village, given the widespread reliance on horse-drawn machinery – a situation which persisted until the 1930s.

A small gathering outside William Foster's post office in Leven. There appears to be some kind of celebration going on: by the fashions, it may be Peace Day in July 1919. In the window of the post office is a patriotic picture of Lord Kitchener, whose moustachioed face was the symbol of the early war years.

The Square, Leven, where North, South, East and West Streets meet. In the centre is one of the North Eastern Railway's buses, while on the right is the grocer's and draper's shop of William Garton. The Hare and Hounds pub is in the background.

Houseboats on the Leven Canal near Sandholme. John Thurlow's Sandholme Farm can be seen in the right background, and the houses of the village are just visible on the left. The canal was built in 1802 from Leven to the River Hull, by Mrs Bethell of Rise Park, to ship out corn and to bring in coal and lime. It ceased to be a navigable waterway in 1936.

Tickton Main Street, looking eastwards. If the man with the stick is not alert, he will be run down by the rapidly approaching cyclist! This was the main road between Beverley and Hornsea; the volume of traffic was clearly then no problem. Again, only the construction of a bypass has returned the Main Street to something approaching this condition.

Hull Bridge, looking south. The River Hull marks the westernmost boundary of Holderness for much of its length. This small industrial settlement grew up at the end of the eighteenth century around this bridge over the river. Visible here is Robert Stephenson's factory, which made artificial fertilizers, and The Crown and Anchor pub. The mansard roof of the cottage in the centre is an unusual feature in local houses, especially in such a small building.

HORNSEA

Model and full-size boats on Hornsea Mere, the largest natural lake in Yorkshire. The Mere, once famous for its pike and perch, was opened for boating and fishing in 1890 by the Constable family, who had owned the fowling and fishing rights since the sixteenth century. This picture is looking along the shoreline, past the boat-house, and towards the distant church.

Looking westwards along Westgate. The grounds of the mid-Victorian Westgate House are to the right.

The Round House, Seaton Road. Also known as The Mushroom Cottage, it dates from 1812. It is not known why the building was erected in this particular style; it may have been no more than an architectural whim, or possibly it made use of a circular threshing floor as a foundation.

Hornsea station, early 1950s. George Hudson's York and North Midland Railway arrived in 1864, bringing holiday-makers from Hull, and taking commuters into the city. An attempt to build a second line, connecting the town with Driffield, never got off the ground. The engine, no. 67371, is a C12 class 4–4–2T, built originally for the Great Northern Railway.

R. Page Loten's shop on Newbegin. It was established in 1860, and Loten was registered with the Worshipful Company of Plumbers of London. The family also had a chemist's shop next door. Plumbers were much in demand before and after the First World War, as water closets, domestic gas and electricity were introduced into many private dwellings.

Eastgate, looking out of town. It is one of the principal thoroughfares of the old town. The village at one time only ran along the edge of the Mere, with a few houses along Eastgate and Newbegin. Even the discovery of a mineral spring near the Mere in the late eighteenth century failed to attract many people to Hornsea to take the waters.

Eastgate again, looking in the opposite direction. One person who did move to Hornsea in the 1840s was a Hull timber merchant, John Ward, who built himself a large house, Hornsea House, in Eastgate. Ward was instrumental in developing the resort during the 1860s. His house was subsequently demolished (the site was used for Hornsea School); nos 11 and 17 are the former lodges to the estate.

St Nicholas's Church from Eastgate. The ditch in the foreground is the site of the former rectory house. Bought by Peter Acklam, the lord of the manor, in 1651, it was demolished in about 1687 and replaced by the Old Hall on the Market Place. The vicarage is out of the picture to the left.

The Rose and Crown, on the Market Place. The landlord was Louis Coley. It was a tied house of Glossop's Brewery of Hull (taken over by the Hull Brewery in 1920).

The Old Hall, built by Peter Acklam to replace the rectory manor-house. At this time it was occupied by Captain Frederick Charles Strickland-Constable, whose family had inherited the lordship of the manor from the Acklam. He was probably responsible for the addition of the square bay windows on either side of the door.

MISS ROSE CARR. HORNSEA.

A noted Hornsea character, Rose Carr. She was born in North Frodingham in 1843, the daughter of John Carr, a farmer. She moved to Hornsea, where she set up as a carrier and coach proprietor; she also provided a taxi service, which was used by local doctors and clergymen on their rounds. She was known as a very strong woman, and early in her life had been a heavy drinker; but she was later to become a Primitive Methodist lay preacher. She was also very good with horses, and was often called upon for her veterinary skills by other owners; ironically, it may have been a horse that kicked her in the head as a child, producing a paralysis of the left side of her face. This picture may have been taken at Hornsea Show – her pony and trap is in immaculate condition.

Southgate, looking towards the corner of Newbegin and the Market Place. Among the shops visible here are those of T.B. Anderson, watch and clock maker, and in the distance Robert Barr, plumber and glazier.

Southgate, with one of the entrances on to Back Southgate on the left. William Lill, whose premises can be seen on the right, was a miller as well as a corn factor, with a mill on Atwick Lane.

Southgate, a little further out of town than the previous picture. The wall on the right is that of the cemetery. The building on the left was known as The White House or Low Hall. Built by the lord of the manor, Peter Acklam, in 1674, it had been a pub before becoming a temperance hotel in 1875. John Clappison Harker had been a cowkeeper before he opened the stables signposted on the wall. The cross in the centre of the picture is of medieval origin, although the shaft is more modern.

Looking out along Newbegin towards the Congregational chapel at the junction with Cliff Lane. It was built in 1872–4 by the Hull architect Samuel Musgrave, and had seats for 500 worshippers. On the left can be seen the Wesleyan chapel, built in 1870 at a cost of £1,660, by another Hull architect, J.K. James, with 400 seats. Remarkably, these two chapels between them could accommodate virtually half the town's population at that time.

Cliff Lane, soon to become Cliff Road, looking northwards. The road was part of the later resort development, and was laid out in about 1900. The Grosvenor Estate, around Eastbourne Road, was the first of these developments. Originally laid out in about 1865, it was slow to be completed. Note the gas lamp on the right: the town was lit by gas produced by a private company's gasworks on Lelley Lane, built in 1866, at a cost of £3,000. The west side of Cliff Road remained undeveloped until the 1970s.

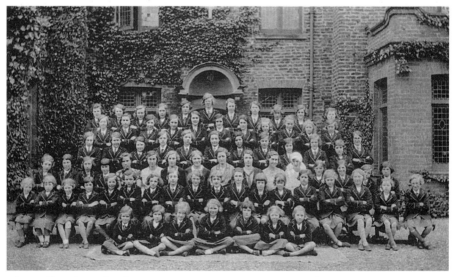

The staff and pupils of Hornsea College. It was opened in the Old Hall in the early 1920s as a boarding and day school, advertising 'a sound education', a gymnasium, and 'moderate' fees. The first principal was Miss F.G. Watson.

Mrs Green and a group of girls from the Newlands Home in Hull, 1908. The orphanage was set up by the Port of Hull Society for the Religious Instruction of Seamen in 1838, and opened its first home on the Newland Estate on Cottingham Road in 1895. They were given a holiday home on Cliff Road in 1908 by Sir James Reckitt, and from the postmark on this postcard, this must have been one of the first groups to go there. The sender of the card, Lizzie Peacock, is somewhere in this group; the other woman may be Miss Brown, the matron.

A children's sports day on the Promenade Gardens. Judging by the adult fashions, it is taking place just after the First World War.

A full ladies' hockey team (eleven players and two reserves) on a postcard posted in Hornsea in 1905. Sadly, their identities remain unknown. Note the extravagant tam-o'-shanters, which were a standard part of a hockey player's kit at that time.

Granville Court, called on this postcard The Hydro, was built by a Hull industrialist in 1914. The sender of the card, Isabel, confessed to her friend Edith in Brighouse that she was having a 'ripping time'. The building was demolished in 1990.

The opening of the Promenade Gardens was performed by Mrs A. Stanley Wilson, the wife of the Conservative MP for Holderness, 6 July 1906. Mrs Wilson was accompanied by her husband and by members of the council.

The boating lake in the Promenade Gardens, late 1940s. The sea wall of 1907 was extended to north and south in 1923, and provision was made for a swimming pool.

A view along the Promenade before the construction of the sea defences. In the background stands the Marine Hotel, dating from 1837. Though much altered subsequently, partly due to the erosion of the cliffs (it was rebuilt in 1874 and again in 1900), it is still there today.

A combination of a spring tide and high winds had a catastrophic effect on the Promenade on 12 March 1906, washing a considerable part away. The wooden barrier provided no kind of defence against such powerful natural forces.

The havoc wreaked by the storm on the flimsy wooden sea defences. It was not the first time that the sea had caused damage on the sea front here, for it had earlier destroyed Hornsea Pier. The pier was finished in the summer of 1880, nearly bankrupting the company that built it. But in October of the same year, a great storm blew up along the east coast, and the ship *The Earl of Derby*, running before the heavy weather, struck and demolished most of the structure. It was never rebuilt.

The rebuilt Promenade. Just visible in the background is the Floral Hall, and the sign pushed into the sand states that it offers teas, coffee, ices and light refreshments 'daintily served'. Everyone here seems to be enjoying the best ingredients of the traditional British seaside holiday – sun, sea and sand, not to mention the donkeys. The people on the beach all appear to be looking out to sea – perhaps a boat is coming inshore.

Further away from the centre of town there was no sea wall. There are plenty of beach shelters in sight here, to keep off the late afternoon sun, or the onshore breezes.

The Reps Concert Party, Hornsea, 1923. This was one of the many pierrot troupes which performed at all the resorts on the Yorkshire coast.

Harry Russell's Naval Cadets were another pierrot troupe. Russell, seated third from the left, was born in Grimsby in 1877, and was involved with a number of different troupes before forming the Cadets for the 1907 season. They normally performed at the north end of the Promenade. Missing from this shot is the sole woman of the troupe, Miss Verna Reed; the others are (left to right) Dickie Tubb, Ernie Harcourt, Russell, Walter Gordon, Bert Gordon and Neville Delmar.

It may be summer and this may be the beach, but these are not sufficient reasons for these grown-ups to wear anything but the most severe dark clothes. The children are rather luckier.

The steam trawler *Witham* of Boston ran aground in a blinding snowstorm south of Hornsea, on the night of 17 January 1905. The conditions prevented the coastguard station from sighting the ship, and the crew had to make their own way ashore.

CENTRAL VILLAGES

Crossroads at Mappleton, looking east towards the coast. The building in the background is the post office, run by the sub-postmistress, Mrs Mary Ann Butler. The sea is encroaching rapidly in this area – it has gained about 1,000 feet since 1786.

The Grimsby steam trawler *Drake* ashore at Mappleton, 13 February 1905. In the foreground is the Hornsea lifeboat. She had been launched to come to the *Drake's* assistance, but although the coxswain brought the boat alongside, the crew refused to abandon ship. As the boat was coming about to return to base, it was caught beam end on by a wave and turned turtle. Most of the lifeboat's crew were thrown overboard, but the coxswain stayed at his post, and was still there when the boat righted.

North Cliffs at Cowden, between the wars. This photograph amply demonstrates the fragile nature of the cliff face in this area, and the farm buildings appear to be in great danger of toppling over the edge of the cliff. They may even be part of the village of Great Cowden itself, which was lost to the sea earlier this century. The sea off Cowden is now a bombing and gunnery range for the RAF.

Rise Rectory, now Rise Park, built in 1809. The incumbent at the time of the photograph was the Revd Joseph Chatto Lamb. The village of Rise no longer occupies its original site – it was moved in the late eighteenth century to make way for the park of Rise Hall, the home of the Bethell family, who were lords of this manor as well as a considerable number of others in the area.

Skirlaugh post office, which was actually in South Skirlaugh. The postmaster was Francis Swift. Letters were received from Hull twice a day, at 6 a.m. and 6 p.m., and they were dispatched at 6.15 a.m. The sign on the left advertises Henry Horner, a plumber and glazier of Sproatley, while those in the window advertise a forthcoming athletic sports contest, Hudson's soap, Peek Frean biscuits and Zebra grate polish.

St Margaret's Church, Long Riston, restored in 1851 and 1887. It is built from cobblestone and brick. In *Buildings of England: York & the East Riding* (1972) Pevsner condemned it as 'rough', but this forthright judgement has been edited out of the new edition.

The post office at Swine, with a very appropriate sign. The village originally grew up around a twelfth-century Cistercian nunnery, but the buildings of the village date from the 1860s, when the Crown purchased the estate and instituted a major programme of rebuilding and remodelling, completed by 1872.

Withernwick Hall. This farm building, constructed in the late eighteenth century, lies just north of the village. The farmer at this time was John Wright, and this may be his wife and child.

Aldbrough Church. This is a very old foundation – an inscription on the south aisle of the north wall reveals that it was built for a Dane called Ulf and his wife, Gunwaru. Much of what remains is thirteenth-century work.

The George Hotel (now the George and Dragon), Aldbrough. It has a very decorative doorway, and offers 'good stabling and cycle storage'. Opposite is the village smithy, and on the right of the picture is the village post office. A sign points 'To The Sea' along Headland Road.

The Royal Hotel, formerly the Spa Inn, looking back towards the coastguard station, Aldbrough cliff top. The hotel was run by Mrs Dinah Evison. The discovery of a mineral spring in 1845 encouraged the development of a seaside resort here, and although it flourished for a time, the collapse of the mud cliffs (see the next picture) and the absence of a railway connection to the wider world meant that the 'resort' collapsed (literally, in the case of the hotel, which has fallen into the sea).

The cliffs at Aldbrough, showing further evidence of their fragile nature. In the foreground, some wooden stairs run down to the shore.

Burton Constable Hall, the home of the Constable family, viewed from the front (above), and from the rear (below). The original hall was built in the last quarter of the sixteenth century, but was much altered from 1759 to 1760. The interior is almost wholly Georgian. Unusually for the landed gentry of the Riding, the Constables remained a Catholic family throughout the religious upheavals of the sixteenth and seventeenth centuries. Nothing now remains of the settlement of Burton Constable, a deserted village, abandoned during the Middle Ages.

The southern end of the lake at Burton Constable Hall. The landscaping work was done by the celebrated landscape gardener Capability Brown between 1769 and 1782. The lakes replaced a chain of fishponds, and were dug out by workmen paid between 2*d* and 5*d* per cubic yard of soil removed.

The Holderness Hunt in typical Holderness countryside. The hunt is held to have been founded in 1726. The first master was William Draper of Beswick, though the hunt was formed around the Bethell hounds, which were kennelled at Low Hall, Bishop Burton. After the First World War, the Holderness Country was split into the Wolds side and the Holderness side, divided by the River Hull, but has since been reunited.

The village green in Sproatley. On the right is George Mumby's, 'Grocers, Provision Dealers, Flour and Offal Merchant', with an impressive array of advertisements on the wall. The building later became the village post office. In the background are the Constable Arms and C. Smith's tailor's.

A cricket match between a team of ladies and a team of gentlemen, part of Sproatley's Peace Day celebrations, 19 July 1919.

The Endowed School, Sproatley. It was endowed in 1773 by a Mrs Bridget Briggs, who left rents and some interest, about £330 a year, for the education of fourteen boys and fourteen girls. Her endowment also gave them £2 10s on leaving school, and a similar sum for the first year after that. The building shown here was built in 1868, and its headmaster at this time was Mr John T. Salisbury.

St Peter's Church, Bilton. It was built to replace an older church in 1852 by G.T. Andrews, the York railway architect, for the Hon. Lydia Dawnay, the lady of the manor.

Wawne ferry over the River Hull. The crossing, together with land supporting it, was owned by the Cistercian abbey at Meaux during the Middle Ages. Meaux Abbey, a daughter house of Fountains, was founded in about 1150 by William le Gros, Count of Aumale and Lord of Holderness. By the thirteenth century, it had acquired large landholdings in the area, including the site of the town of Hull, then called Wyke. After the Dissolution of the Monasteries in 1539, it was demolished and the stones used in Hull's town defences.

Wawne, looking westward past the thirteenth-century church of St Peter. Wawne Hall is hidden by the trees. The modern village is a little way to the north of the medieval settlement, which became the site of two farms. Wawne was owned by the Windham family from the late seventeenth century until the sale of the estate in 1911. Wawne Hall itself was built in the eighteenth century, and demolished in the 1950s.

Ganstead Mill, pre-1909. This post mill was demolished in 1909; it is certainly looking rather dilapidated in the picture. The last occupant was probably George Jubb, who was milling here in 1905. Note there are two different types of sail – an unusual arrangement. The mill was equipped with two pairs of so-called 'French' mill-stones, a type which had originally come from the town of La Ferté-sous-Jouarre, near Paris, and was particularly used for making fine-grade flour.

St Margaret's Church, Hilston, and Church Farm. The church was rebuilt by Sir Tatton Sykes in 1862. It could seat eighty people, but the population of the village in 1901 was only twenty-nine. It was destroyed by a bomb in 1941, and has been replaced by a new building. The farmhouse is now a private dwelling called The Gables.

Looking northwards up Danthorpe Road in Humbleton. The school is the building on the right; it is now a private house.

Class C at Humbleton School. The school buildings were built in 1878 for 121 children, but the school itself had first been endowed in 1718 by a Francis Heron with 50 acres in Flinton, which produced some £80 a year. The teacher was Miss Jane Catherine Hanger (the lady on the right).

Church Street, Sutton, looking westwards. In the background is the Wesleyan chapel, 'one of the most pleasing in the Riding', built in 1859. From 1929 Sutton was absorbed by the spreading conurbation of Hull, but although largely surrounded by the Bransholme Estate, it has still managed to retain a recognizable village centre. During the nineteenth and early twentieth centuries, it attracted many wealthy Hull residents.

Church Street again. The Ship Inn was run by William Reader. Next door is Taylor's shop, which also served as the post office. Sutton Church was built in the fourteenth and fifteenth centuries partly in brick, like Holy Trinity in Hull. It was run not by a single parish priest but by a college of canons, which is a reflection of the wealth of the Sutton family, who are commemorated inside the church.

Looking westwards along Kirk Lane, from Rectory Lane, towards the church, Preston. All Saints' Church is built largely of cobbles, and contains some thirteenth-century elements. It was restored from 1878 to 1882 by the Hull architects Smith and Brodrick; Cuthbert Brodrick also designed Leeds Town Hall.

School Lane, from the junction with Main Street, Preston. The old Council School is partly hidden by the tree on the right. It opened in 1877, with room for 233 children, and closed during the 1970s, to be replaced by a new building on Station Road. Just visible on the left are the roofs of the Primitive Methodist chapel and its Sunday School.

Preston United Football Club, *c.* 1910. The man in the centre of the middle row is Tom Warn.

Looking southwards down Main Street, Preston, from Town End. In the distance are the buildings of Manor Farm. Hidden by the houses on the right is the Order of Druids' lodge building, for the T.W. Flint Lodge, no. 472 – one of the many friendly society lodges which could be found in every village during the nineteenth century. Friendly Societies were an important aspect of village life in the days before the Welfare State, providing sickness and life insurance.

Looking towards High Paull and the Battery. The lighthouse was built in 1836 by Hull Trinity House, and was in use until 1870, when it was replaced by two lights to the south-east and two more at Saltend.

The soldiers' quarters at Paull. A battery had originally been built here for the defence of the Humber approaches to Hull in 1542; the present work dates from 1861 to 1864. It was used by the local Artillery Volunteers for practice, and as the centre of an operation to mine the Humber in case of war. The guns were later taken out and replaced by a powerful searchlight.

St Andrew's Church, Paull. Separate from the village, it was built on its elevated site in about 1355, after the previous church had been washed away by the Humber. This church has also suffered – but at the hands of man, for it was burned in 1643, during the siege of Hull.

Town Street, Paull. On the right is the Humber Tavern and on the left is The Crown. The proprietor of the former was trying to encourage visitors from Hull in 1808, with the attraction of a bathing machine and views of a nearby shipyard. The Crown was a comparative latecomer, opening in about 1865.

The foreshore at Paull, with a well-loaded keel making her way downriver. The buildings of Hull can just be seen on the left.

A driving test at Thorngumbald Show, 1905. The object appears to be to steer this donkey and cart around the line of bottles, without knocking them over. The origin of the singular village name lies in the combination of the word for 'thorn tree' with the name of the family who were the medieval lords of the manor, which medieval scribes managed to spell (or mis-spell) as Gumbaud, Grimbald, Gobaud, or even Grimbeard.

Another view taken at the show, this time of a pony trap belonging to G. Sergeant. The show originally took place in a field called Furdales (now a market garden). It fell into abeyance until the late 1940s, when it was most successfully revived, although held in a different location (now Summergangs Road and Grange Road Junior School). It is now part of Gala Day, which takes place on land behind The Crescent.

Thorngumbald Hall. It was built in about 1770 by Samuel Standidge, a Hull man, who had made his money in the whaling trade, using bricks from the old hospital at Newton Garth. It was rebuilt in 1881 for Charles Hargitt Johnson, a Hull businessman. It is now a residential home for the elderly.

HEDON

A view from the church tower looking eastwards along Magdalen Gate (now part of Baxter Gate). On the left is the yard for Webster's Hull and Hedon horse buses, which ran from the nearby King's Head to The Tally Ho pub in Bond Street.

Looking northwards this time. Market Hill is on the left, and in the distance is the station yard and the end of Soutter Gate, where some house-building is under way. Just visible through the haze to the north is the village of Preston. The narrowness of the building plots reflects the original layout of the town in the Middle Ages.

St Augustine's Church, the 'King of Holderness'. The original caption to the picture above states that this is how the church appeared in 1870, but it may be slightly earlier, since G.E. Street's restoration of the church actually started in 1867. Note the house within the churchyard – this was occupied by the vicar, even though there was a vicarage in Soutter Gate. The picture below (post-1883) shows the effect of the restoration work. It was finally completed in 1876, although more work was done on the tower from 1881 to 1883.

A quiet conversation on Soutter Gate, outside Emily Calvert's Station Hotel. It was originally named The Sun, but changed to The Durham Ox in about 1852, and to The Station Hotel in 1880. The man on the right is a policeman. The Borough of Hedon once employed a number of constables, but policing was taken over by the East Riding force in 1858. The police station was on St Augustine's Gate – it is now the site of the public library.

Another view along Soutter Gate. On the right is George Scott's draper's shop. Note the decorative quoins of the house next door, no. 45. It was built in the mid-nineteenth century. The name Soutter Gate means 'the street of the leather sewers'; coincidentally, a local family called Soutter lived here at one time, and it may have been their presence which saw the alteration of the old spelling, Souter Gate, to the current form, with a double 't'.

A delivery in progress, of Darley's Thorne Ales, to The Rose and Crown, on the corner of Fletcher Gate. The landlord at this time was George Lonsdale. Although classed as a beerhouse, which did not normally have rooms to let, the pub sign indicates that it offered accommodation to cyclists as well. Fletcher Gate was originally Flesher (i.e. Butcher) Gate, and had nothing to do with fletchers, who made arrows.

St Augustine's Gate, with the Town Hall on the right, and the Sun Inn on the left. The Town Hall was built in 1693 at the expense of Henry Guy, one of the town's MPs at that time. The original name of this street was St Augustine Gate – somewhere it has picked up an extra 's'. Hedon had two MPs until the Reform Act of 1832, when it was disenfranchized because of the small size of the electorate, and amalgamated into the Holderness Division of the East Riding Constituency.

The Peace Day parade of 19 July 1919 winds its way down St Augustine's Gate, past the Town Hall. Veterans are at the front here, with one man still in his uniform, followed by two policemen, the mayor, Councillor R.A. Park, Howard Markham carrying the town mace, a group of nurses, and then the town's schoolchildren.

The Market Place. In front is James Soutter's grocer's, and on the left another grocery, that of Charles Wright. Next door to him is Leonard Wright's butcher's. The shop on the right-hand side may be Alice Johnson's confectioner's, advertising its own ice-cream and Kop's American Cream Drink.

Scrambling for pennies outside the Town Hall, 1953. This is a traditional part of the annual mayor-making ceremony – it probably goes back to the nineteenth century when bribery at election time was commonplace. Before the First World War the new mayor also used to distribute fruit, but food shortages brought that to an end.

Baxter Gate, by the corner with George Street (which is just out of the picture to the left), just before the First World War. Baxter Gate was 'the street of the female bakers', a name acquired during the fourteenth century. The part north of Grape Lane was known as Magdalen Gate until quite recently.

Burgess Square, off Baxter Gate, with three of Hedon's older residents of the time, sadly unidentified. The houses here were called the Burrage Houses, and were almshouses built in 1812, with much of the cost defrayed by the town's two MPs. The inhabitants lived there rent-free with an annual gift of wood and coal for the winter. The houses were demolished in the early 1970s.

Baxter Gate again, with the Shakespeare Inn on the left. The landlord was Thomas Massey. This hostelry was originally named the Charles Saunders Inn, after a Hedon MP of the eighteenth century, but changed its name in about 1880.

An earlier picture of the Shakespeare, pre-1904. Arthur Wardell, seen here with his wife, was landlord until about 1904. Note the bust of the bard on the gable end, beneath the sign.

George Street. The terrace of houses on the left were all built in about 1888. On the other side of the road is the Wesleyan chapel, built in 1818, but rebuilt in 1875, with seating for 250 people. It was deconsecrated after the Second World War, and was subsequently used as public rooms.

Ivy House from Ivy Lane. The pond on the left was called the Horse Well. The house was built in the eighteenth century, but is more noted for the pieces of stonework in the garden, rescued from churches that were being restored. They came mostly from Owthorne and Kilnsea, but fragments were also acquired from Hull, Beverley, Marfleet, Hedon and Hollym. The small building on the left is the so-called tomb of Drogo de Beuvrière, Lord of Holderness in the eleventh century, but it was in fact built in about 1810.

Holyrood House and the Kilnsea Cross. Holyrood was planned as an elegant square by James Iveson, but only two houses were built in about 1820; they were knocked into one and extended in 1885. The cross is supposed to have been erected to commemorate the landing of King Henry IV at Ravenser in 1399, at the start of his campaign to secure the throne. It was washed up at Kilnsea in 1818, and was erected here in 1828.

Sheriff Highway, which was the road to the Sheriff Bridge over the Haven. It was also known as Westgate during the fourteenth century, as Mill Lane during the eighteenth century, and more recently as Havenside or Paull Road.

The Haven. Hedon was founded by the Counts of Aumale during the twelfth century as a port with ready access to the Humber, with as many as three havens to accommodate ships. But the rise of both Hull and Ravenser Odd on the Spurn Peninsula affected Hedon's trade badly, and the silting up of the havens during the Middle Ages finished it off completely.

The yellow buses of Robert Laidlaw, 1923. The one on the left is a Vulcan, while the other two are Ford Baico T-types. The service started just after the First World War, using a box on wheels, with straw on the floor, but it soon improved after these machines were introduced. The fare from Hedon to the terminus near the Cecil, in Carr Lane, was 6d. The firm was taken over by East Yorkshire Motor Services in 1926.

The station. It was opened in June 1854 on the Hull–Withernsea line of the Hull and Holderness Railway Company. There were four trains a day in each direction. The company did not last very long – it was leased in perpetuity to the North Eastern Railway in 1862. The line was closed in 1968, as part of the Beeching cuts. The railway had a profound effect on the town's economy, making it easier and cheaper to take goods in and out of the area, to Hull and Beverley, than it was to sell them within the town itself.

Hedon's volunteer firemen with the mayor, J.J. ('Johnnie') Warn, and Alderman Alfred Tinkler, *c.* 1940. At least two of these men can be positively identified – William Hales and Len Sharpe are the first and the fifth firemen on the left respectively. Both men were later to become mayor of the town.

The Holderness Hunt. The man on the right is Major Clive Wilson of Tranby Croft, who was master from 1915 until his death in 1921. His father, Arthur Wilson, had been master before him, from 1878 to 1905.

Hedon Races, and all eyes are fixed on the horses as they head for the winning post. Despite the crowds here, among them a Leeds bookmaker, the course was not a success, and only fifteen meetings were held between 1885 and 1909, before the Race Company folded, and the course was closed.

After the failure of the race company, the racecourse was used as an airfield. On 13 July 1912, the German aviator Gustav Hamel flew in, to be met by the mayors of Hedon and Hull, and a large crowd of spectators. He made three brief flights over the surrounding countryside, before the display was curtailed by cloudy weather. Hamel returned the following week for several other demonstration flights.

A cricket team in black face. The badges on the caps indicate that they are members of Hedon Cricket Club.

South Holderness Cricket Club, 1st XI, 1913. Back row, left to right: Michael Storey, Eddie Drescher, John Hurd, Rex Watkinson, Mr Featherstone (?), -?-, Alderman John Heron, Reg Casson. Middle row: Mr Fenner, Wilf Fewson, Arthur Moforth, Harry Fewson. Front row: William Heron, Tony Iveson, William Henry Warn.

Hedon School Football Club, 1923–4 season. Back row, left to right: Mr Clark (butcher), -?-, Percy Woodford, W.P. Everingham, -?-, -?-, -?-, -?-, -?-, Billy Heron, Mr Markham, 'Wiz' Hopper, -?-, -?-, -?-. Middle row: Oliver ?, Harry Norrison, -?-, Bob Smith, Cliff (?) Everingham. Front row: ? Brunney, Steve ?, ? Thompson, -?-, Rufus Hewetson, -?-.

A brass band. There were a number of itinerant German bands which played at local fairs in the period before the First World War, but the anti-German feeling engendered at the outbreak of that conflict brought their activities to a halt. More formal brass bands were a common feature in the bigger villages and towns throughout the second half of the nineteenth century.

83

Waiting for the parade to begin at the school feast, 1910. Ivy House is in the background. A large number of feasts took place in the summer months, organized by the Sunday Schools (of the Church of England, the Primitive Methodists or the Wesleyan Methodists), or by a number of the friendly societies which had lodges in the town – the Samaritans (which ceased in 1897), the Oddfellows, the Foresters, the Girls' Friendly Society, the Band of Hope and the Sons of Temperance.

A fine collection of hats at the school feast, 1910. Feasts were often the occasion for children's sports, and this seems to be the case here, with everyone being held back by a rope.

An Aunt Sally at one of the school feasts. The original form of the game involved throwing sticks, such as those on the table in front of the doll, in an attempt to hit either a pipe held in the doll's mouth or just the head itself. The origins are obscure; it may be distantly connected with some form of animal-baiting. The expression 'Aunt Sally' in this context dates only from the mid-nineteenth century.

The school feast parade reaches the Market Place. The Dog and Duck is in the background. After forming up outside the church, the parade would march through the streets of the town, before returning to Market Hill. The cobbles in the Market Place have been the subject of controversy over the past few years; the last cobbles elsewhere in the town were removed from Soutter Gate in 1934.

Forming up for the school feast, 1914. The boys at the front probably belong to the Hull Sailor's Orphanage Brass Band, which played at a number of feasts in the area before the First World War.

School feast, 1913. The fourth lady from the left is Miss Petch; standing next to her dressed in white is Miss Gibson, and the other two ladies are Mrs Wilden Thompson and Mrs Dean. Leading Billie Heron's pony and trap is Jack Curtis. Also visible on this picture is Rex Ainslie (in the flat cap on the right), Mr Gibb (in the boater) and Arthur Iveson (the boy by the pony's head).

Mr S. Jones, the Hedon photographer, c. 1890. He lived in Soutter Gate, where he also had a fish-frying business.

A scene at Hedon Show, which took place annually in Fewson's Fields. Arthur Fewson, who lived at the Old Hall, was a dealer and a prize-winning breeder of hackney horses towards the end of the nineteeenth century. He bought promising horses from local farmers, before preparing them for sale to London dealers at the big horse fair at Horncastle, in Lincolnshire.

Section Five

WITHERNSEA

Withernsea lighthouse was built by London Trinity House in 1892–4 on Hull Road, opposite the end of Arthur Street. It was closed in 1976, but remains as a landmark. It contains a small museum, with an exhibit dedicated to the actress and singer Kay Kendall, who was born in the town. This picture is looking westwards along Hull Road.

The Convalescent Home, built by the North Eastern Railway as the Queen's Hotel in 1855. They sold it to the local Improvement Company in 1881, but the latter went into liquidation, and it was finally closed down in 1892. The building was then bought by the Hull industrialists and philanthropists Francis and James Reckitt, given to the Hull Royal Infirmary, and opened as a convalescent home the following year. It has since become a general hospital.

Patients of the Convalescent Home, 1910. There was room for thirty patients. The matron at this time was Miss M. Jackson.

The annexe shown here was added to the Convalescent Home as a sanatorium for tuberculosis patients in 1902, again the gift of James Reckitt, and became a full part of the HRI in 1923. Fresh air was considered to be the cure for this complaint, and being situated on the coast Withernsea had that in abundance. The annexe is now a health centre.

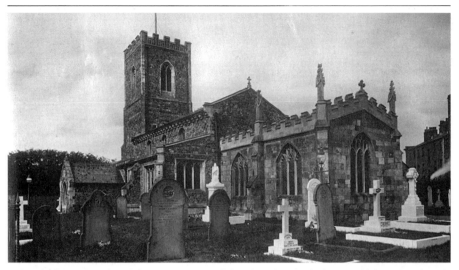

St Nicholas's Church, Withernsea. Most of the church is built from cobbles. The church was rebuilt by Cuthbert Brodrick in 1858–9 around the shell of the old church, which had lost its roof in a storm and had been abandoned some time after 1609. The medieval church, St Mary's, had been washed into the sea in the fifteenth century.

The Queen's Hotel. This was the second establishment of this name – the first had become the Convalescent Home. This building was erected between 1898 and 1901 on Queen Street South, on the corner with Cheverton Avenue. Behind it, on the right-hand side, is the Congregational church, built in 1902, with room for 150 worshippers.

This terrace of houses on Queen Street was known as Sunny Bank. The building with the pinnacled tower on the right-hand side stands opposite the second Queen's Hotel, shown in the previous picture.

High Brighton Street, looking towards Hollym Road. Most of the development that took place in Withernsea in the 1890s was based around existing streets, but this street, along with Cheverton and Lee Avenues, was laid out from scratch. The ground on the right has now become part of the gardens on Queen's Promenade.

Pier Road ran straight from the railway station to the pier, so that holiday-makers could get to the beach as quickly as possible. The war memorial has since been moved. The railway was the source of most of the town's prosperity as a resort (the same applied to Hornsea), for it was this which brought holiday-makers in sufficient numbers to justify the town's outlay on facilities.

The Central Promenade, looking northwards. On the left is the fence around the Valley Gardens and Seaside (spelt here on the distant street sign as two words) Road.

The Central Promenade. It was constructed in 1911, on either side of the old pier entrance. The pier itself was built in 1877, and was originally 1,196 feet long. It was reduced to about 300 feet by storms in 1893, and to 50 feet four years later. Despite an attempt to rebuild it in 1901, all that remained four years later were the castellated entrance towers. On the left, a pierrot troupe entertain a crowd who, apparently, would much rather stand than sit in the deckchairs provided – you had to pay to sit down!

The same spot on the Promenade during the 1920s. The pierrots have gone, but the swings are still there, and there are now at least four different ice-cream sellers vying for custom.

The bandstand on the North Promenade. It was originally built in 1901, but later had to be lowered, because its wooden legs were beginning to show signs of rot.

Donkeys on Withernsea beach. These patient, much put-upon animals became a feature of the seaside scene from the end of the nineteenth century.

Part of the celebrations for King George V's Coronation at Withernsea, 22 June 1911. They commenced with an open-air service at the pier steps at 10.30 a.m. The parade seen here then wound its way round the streets of the town, headed by the lifeboat, which was followed by civic dignitaries and the town's schoolchildren. A free tea for the children was provided, followed by a bonfire in the evening.

The north end of the Promenade. The North Prom was started in 1871 by the Withernsea Pier, Promenade, Gas and General Improvement Company. It had not been completed by the time the company went into liquidation, and it was left to the council to improve it. This it did in 1910, later extending the North Prom in 1920.

The end of the North Promenade at North Cliff. The building on the right, with flags flying, is the coastguard station, built in about 1905. It closed in 1951.

Valley Gardens. This was originally a small lake called Withernsea Mere, but it drained away through cliff erosion, and the Council built these gardens in 1910. The surrounding fence is intended as a wind break.

Holmpton Road camp – built as a camp for the Men's, Boys' and Girls' Brigades from all over Yorkshire. This was the dining-room – sleeping accommodation was in bell tents. A more modern chalet-style holiday camp was later built on Holmpton Road.

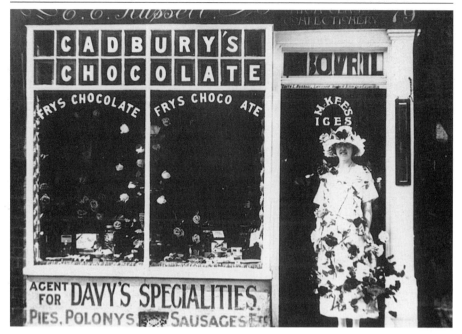

Russell's Confectioner's at 79 Queen Street. It does seem a little unusual for a confectioner to be an agent for pork pies and polony. The lady in front is Mrs Leconby. She appears to be dressed for a carnival, with roses on her dress. There are also roses in the window of the shop.

The scene outside the Committee Rooms of Samuel Savery (later Sir Samuel) during an election, probably the General Election of 1923. He was elected as the Conservative candidate for the Holderness constituency of the East Riding, which he served until his death in 1938.

A carnival procession going along Queen Street, 1920s. In the background is the Kinema, the town's first cinema, built just before the First World War, and owned by Samuel Stratford. There were two other cinemas in the town. The second, the Select, was opened in about 1929 in the Central Hall. It changed its name to the Savoy in 1931. The third cinema was the Cosy, opened just after the Second World War in Queen Street South. All three closed in the 1960s. The Kinema became an amusement arcade.

The wreck of the steam trawler *Leonora*, driven ashore at Withernsea on 6 January 1905, during a night of gales all down the east coast. The crew were all rescued by breeches buoy, launched from the cliffs above.

Are these men a rescued ship's crew? Although they are pictured with men of the coast-guard, they are dressed neither as a rocket apparatus crew nor as lifeboatmen.

SOUTHERN
VILLAGES

Burstwick School. It was built in 1875, with accommodation for 111 pupils, but the average attendance at this time was about 60. Note the curious low-slung trap outside the school. Alfred Webb was the headmaster when these pictures were taken. Is that him standing by the wall behind the children in the picture below? He was assisted by Mrs Fanny Webb, the infants' mistress, and Miss Winifred Webb, assistant mistress – one of them is standing outside the school in the top picture. Such a family connection appears to have been quite common in village schools at this time.

A view northwards along Haroff Lane, by the corner of Newbridge Road, Burstwick. Just off the picture to the left is The Nag's Head. The manor of Burstwick was owned by the Crown, and was used as a base for campaigns against the Scots. The manor-house was used to imprison Robert the Bruce's queen between 1306 and 1308. It was demolished in 1802.

Roos village street, looking northwards, from just past the junction with Hodgson Lane (on the right). The shop on the left is William Johnson's butcher's.

All Saints' Church, Roos, lies a long way beyond the southern end of the modern village, but next to the site of the Roos family manor-house. There was a small chapel of ease in the village centre. The avenue of yew trees was planted in about 1867. Part of the church is of fifteenth-century origin, but the rest dates from a number of Victorian restorations.

Roos Rectory. It was built in 1892 at a cost of £2,720 by the architect Temple Moore. Moore had previously undertaken a lot of church restoration work for Sir Tatton Sykes of Sledmere, and was probably employed here because the Sykes were patrons of the living. The man at the door may be the incumbent, the Revd Edward Milsom.

Dent Garth and the Sunday School, Roos. These two buildings were outside the village, to the eastern side of the hall grounds. The footpath seen here is a continuation of South End Road, and led to the church.

Burton Pidsea, looking south along Church Street. On the left is the school, built in 1872 for 70 pupils, and then enlarged in 1910 to take 110. In front of St Peter's Church is the Nancy Inn, named after a famous racehorse of the 1850s bred by Ned Baxter, who lived in the village. The pub sells Brunt's beer, which was made by a Scunthorpe brewery.

Mount Pleasant, Keyingham. This is not marked on contemporary maps, but we are at the back of St Nicholas's Church, looking towards what is now Church Farm, just off Station Road. St Nicholas's Church is in the background. Much of the work is thirteenth century – the village was the location for a farm belonging to Meaux Abbey. The spire was removed in 1969.

The road between Hedon and Patrington as it passes through Keyingham, looking eastwards. The smithy was behind the trees on the left, and in the background is The Blue Bell. In the centre of the road is the stump of an old cross. The former centre of the village has since been overwhelmed by the large number of houses that have been built here within the last thirty years.

The bleak nature of some of the Holderness countryside is shown in this picture, taken near Keyingham. The men on the road are soldiers of the Royal Artillery Volunteers, probably returning from a practice drill on the Humber Banks.

A tranquil, pastoral scene, looking over the fields towards St Wilfred's Church, Ottringham. The village is off the picture to the left. Like Keyingham, Ottringham was also the site of a monastery farm, but in this instance, one belonging to the Priory at Bridlington.

St German's Church, Winestead. The church is notable for the monuments inside to the Hildyard family, who were lords of the manor. The village was the birthplace of the seventeenth-century poet and politician Andrew Marvell, whose father was the incumbent here.

The approach to Winestead Hall. During this period it was the home of Boswell George Jalland, the son of Boswell Middleton Jalland, Mayor of Hull in 1836 and 1846, and the man after whom Jalland Street is named. He lived in Holderness House, on Holderness Road (whose adjoining estate is now Garden Village), but his son moved into the country. The hall, also known as White Hall (there was a Red Hall as well, demolished in 1936), was originally built from 1814 to 1815 for the Maisters, a prominent family of Hull merchants.

Patrington, looking eastwards from the church tower. Kiln Lane is in the foreground, with High Street to the left. In the background are the houses of Marine Place, and the almshouses.

Looking northwards along Pump Row, Patrington. On the right is the post office (postmistress Mrs Christine Pickering), and on the left is the Amicable Society Inn (licensee James Stephenson). The inn also served as the meeting place of the Patrington Amicable Society, founded in 1792. The building is now a private house.

Patrington Church

The magnificent St Patrick's Church, the 'Queen of Holderness'. Most of the church was built between the late thirteenth century and the middle of the fourteenth, no doubt at the behest of the Archbishop of York, who was also the lord of the manor. It replaced an earlier, Norman, edifice. Apart from its elegant lines, it is also noted for its size – almost 150 feet in length. The spire was not added until about 1400; it reaches a height of 180 feet.

Dr William Coates. He arrived in the village in 1891, taking over the practice of a Dr Duffy, and lived at Bleak House, near the church. He died in 1924. Here, he is about to climb into his 10 h.p. Humber. He is wearing the green and gold uniform of the National Motor Volunteers. This was an Army reserve organization, raised after the Boer War, whose members volunteered their services, and their cars, for communications and scouting duties, at a time when the Army had very few motor vehicles.

High Street, Patrington, looking eastwards. In the background is the eighteenth-century Bleak House, with the mock-Tudor addition provided by Dr Coates. On the left is the Holderness Inn (now The Pelican), and on the right is the shop belonging to Mrs Martha Dibnah, who was a tailor. The man on the right has moved during the taking of the photo, leaving a ghostly, transparent image.

Patrington Market Place, looking eastwards. On the right is Mrs Elizabeth Burnham's chemist's, possibly with the lady herself peeping out. Also on that side was Tiplady's boot and shoe shop.

The broad expanse of Westgate, Patrington. It seems possible that this was once part of a much larger market-place, which was bounded by Northside and Pump Row, or even Tithe Barn Lane. It is easy to forget that Patrington was once the major commercial centre for south Holderness, with a flax mill, a small haven, and a population of 1,827 in 1851 (a level which it is only just regaining). Its decline was probably due to the arrival of the railway from Withernsea to Hull, which took virtually all the trade away from the town.

The crew of the Holmpton rocket apparatus, *c.* 1897. This was used to help rescue seamen from ships which had gone ashore, and shot a life-line from the beach or cliff top aboard the vessel. The personnel are a mixture of coastguards and civilian volunteers.

Northside Road, Hollym, with St Nicholas's Church in the background. It was built in 1884, incorporating part of an earlier building of 1814. On the right is the village smithy, and behind that, the Plough Inn.

Maypole dancing at Hollym, 7 July 1908. The dancing was part of the celebrations taking place at the crowning of the May Queen. This was a custom observed in many Holderness villages at one time, but seems largely to have disappeared by the 1950s.

St Mary's Church, Welwick, a mixture of thirteenth- and fourteenth-century work. The church was at the west end of the village, which straggled along the road to Skeffling in one direction, and in the other down towards the Humber Bank, where the hamlet of Orwithfleet was located before being lost to the sea in the fourteenth century.

A scene from the interior of Welwick Church showing a fourteenth-century tomb, possibly that of William de la Mare, provost of Beverley Minster from 1338 to 1360, or perhaps his brother Thomas, vicar of Welwick (died 1358). The carvings are the work of those responsible for the very fine Percy tomb in Beverley Minster – the provost was the lord of the manor of Welwick.

Looking northwards over Easington, with the Dimlington and Skeffling roads stretching into the distance. The land on the right is now the site of the natural gas terminal, while that on the left has been built over. On North Church Street is the Marquis of Granby, and next door is the Sun Inn, which was only a beerhouse. Beerhouses were not licensed to sell spirits; they were thus rather looked down on by inns, while both were looked down on by hotels.

A view looking north-eastwards over Easington from the church tower, looking down Black Well Row to the sea. The horse and trap on North Church Street, probably a milk delivery, carries on oblivious of the photographer. The buildings on the corner, with the tower, were attached to the coastguard station. In the distance, at the junction of the Row with Ten Chains Road, is the Wesleyan Methodist chapel.

High Street, Easington, looking northwards. Note the thatched cottages on the left. In the background is All Saints' Church. Like many of the houses in the village, it is (now only partially) built of cobblestones. The earliest parts of the building date from the twelfth century, but there are contributions dating from virtually every century thereafter.

High Street, Easington, looking southwards. The house on the left is built of cobbles. Cobbles occur naturally on sea shores or in areas of boulder clay, such as Holderness. They are easy to handle and require little processing before use. However, their continuous extraction from the shore only served to aggravate the erosion caused by the wind and the sea. When a prohibition on taking cobbles from the shore was introduced, and a tax on bricks was repealed in 1849, the latter became the dominant building material of the area.

The so-called 'tithe barn', Easington. It may date from the fifteenth or even the sixteenth century, and is part of the Rectory Farm, which during the Middle Ages belonged to Meaux Abbey. It is now the only large, aisled, timber-frame barn in the East Riding, since a smaller one was recently destroyed at Mappleton. Part of the barn was converted, by Hull Museums, into a folklore museum in the 1920s.

Class B at Easington National School. The school opened in 1860, and at this time had an average daily attendance of between 60 and 80 pupils. The headmaster was Edward Anson, and the infants' mistress was Mrs E. Benson.

A Sunday School trip from Easington. The wagon is being drawn by a steam engine. The occasion is perhaps the Wesleyan Sunday School anniversary on 11 July 1906, when there was a trip to Withernsea.

The windmill off Dimlington Road, just outside Easington. A mill was first recorded here in about 1260. This mill remained in use until the 1920s, when it was closed and later demolished.

Easington lifeboat crew, with members of the coastguard and some civilian helpers. The lifeboat station was transferred here from Withernsea in 1913. The boat, the *Docea Chapman*, remained in service until 1933.

Kilnsea Church. The original church was lost to the sea in stages over three hundred years. In 1577 it was described as being neglected, and then in 1699 it was decided to maintain only the east end. All of the church except the tower fell into the sea in 1826, and the latter went the same way five years later. This church was built half a mile to the west of the original site in 1864–5, by A. Burgess. It includes a fourteenth-century font preserved from the original church.

The effects of an inundation by the sea, Kilnsea, 12 March 1900. This view is taken from the Humber Bank, looking eastwards to the sea. A combination of a high tide with a strong north-west wind broke through the sea defences, and as can be seen, cut off the village and Spurn. Kilnsea children could not get to school for almost a week – though it seems unlikely that they minded very much! In the background is Kilnsea beacon, a navigational aid dismantled in 1939.

A group of Spurn children enjoying a winkle-picking contest.

For anyone who enjoyed fresh air, there was plenty to be had on Spurn Point, and it attracted some holiday-makers from the turn of the century. This group has acquired some sheltered accommodation; and judging by the empties, accommodation well supplied by the brewers Bass.

Not everyone appears to have been so lucky – despite the painted sign advertising 'comfortable apartments', these digs seem a little spartan in comparison with the previous picture, not to mention a little windswept. The orchestra is rather short-handed as well.

The new and old lighthouses. The first light on Spurn was erected in 1674 by one Justinian Angel. This was replaced by two lights in 1776. One of these was placed near the tide line, and had to be moved several times over the next hundred years. It was finally abandoned in 1895, and as can be seen in the picture, its base was normally underwater. The light on dry land was built in 1895.

A view of Spurn taken from the new lighthouse. On the right are the old lifeboat cottages, replaced from 1974 to 1975, with the school just to their left. Further behind, and hidden in a fold of the ground, is the lifeboat shed. On the left-hand side is the main signal station, and in the middle background is the signal station belonging to Lloyds of London.

Acknowledgements

For the use of photographs in their collections, we would like to thank Humberside Leisure Services, Barbara Roe, and particularly Martin Craven for all his help and generosity; we are also grateful to the staffs of Beverley Reference Library and Hull Local Studies Library for their help.

High tide at Spurn Point, 1906. The old lighthouse of 1852, used here as an explosives store (probably for flares, maroons, etc.), is completely surrounded by the sea, showing how far the Point has moved since the lighthouse was built.